MUSE

THE 2ND LAW

Music Arranged by Olly Weeks

Edited by Lucy Holliday

Book Design by Chloë Alexander

Neuro images supplied courtesy of the Human Connectome Project, Laboratory of Neuro Imaging, UCLA

Band Photography by Gavin Bond

ISBN 978-1-4768-8937-5

7777 W. BLUEMOUND RD. P.O. BOX 13819 MILWAUKEE, WI 53213

Visit Hal Leonard Online at
www.halleonard.com

muse.mu

Contents

SUPREMACY

Words and Music by Matthew Bellamy

Wake to see, your true e - man - ci - pa - tion is a fan - ta - sy.

Your su - pre - ma - cy.__

MADNESS

Words and Music by Matthew Bellamy

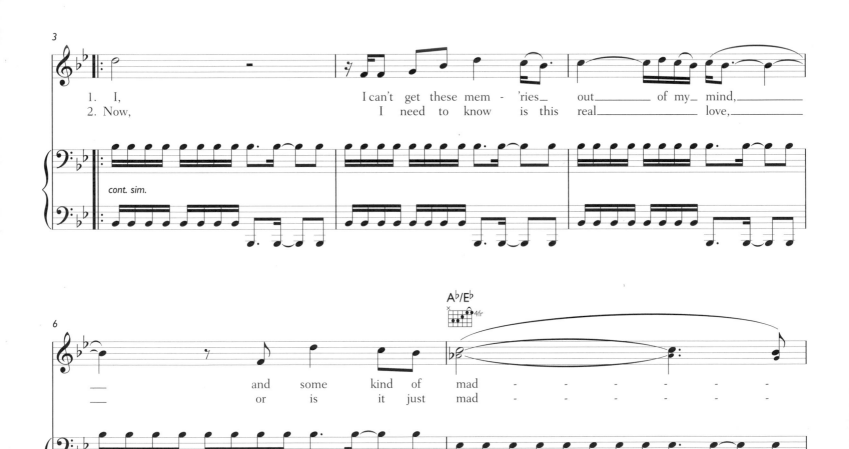

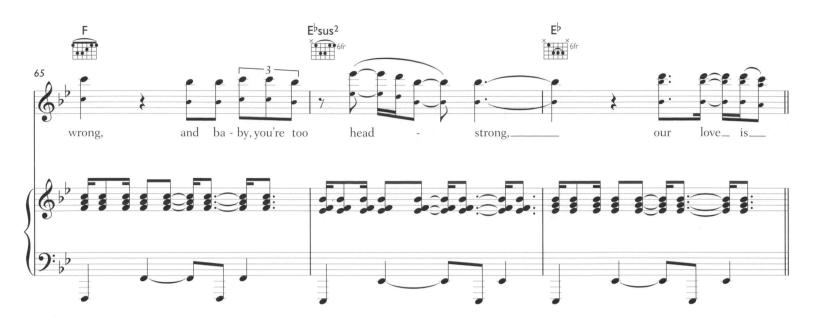

PANIC STATION

Words and Music by Matthew Bellamy

1. You won't get much clos-er____ un-til you sac-ri-fice it all, you won't get to taste it____ with your
2. Doubts will try to break you,____ un-leash your heart and soul, troub-le will sur-round you, start____

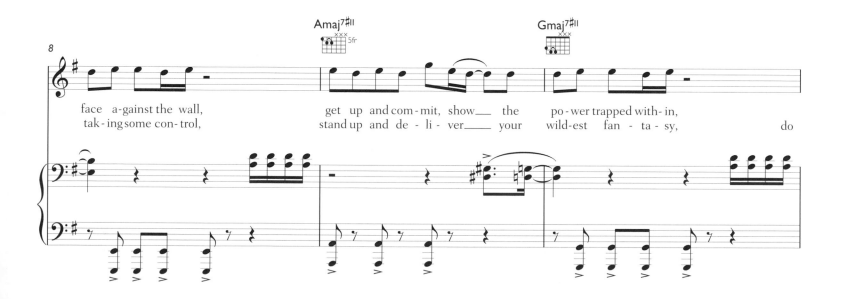

face a-gainst the wall, get up and com-mit, show____ the po-wer trapped with-in, tak-ing some con-trol, stand up and de-li-ver____ your wild-est fan-ta-sy, do

PRELUDE

Words and Music by Matthew Bellamy

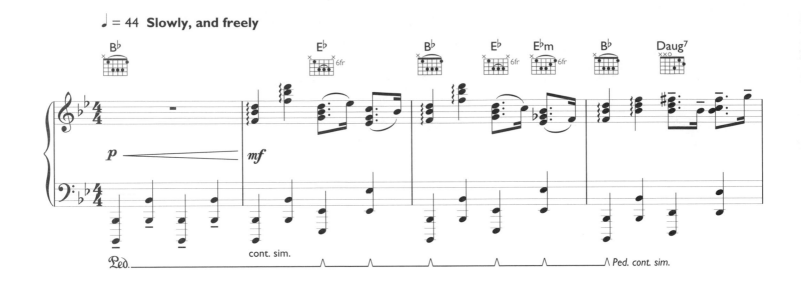

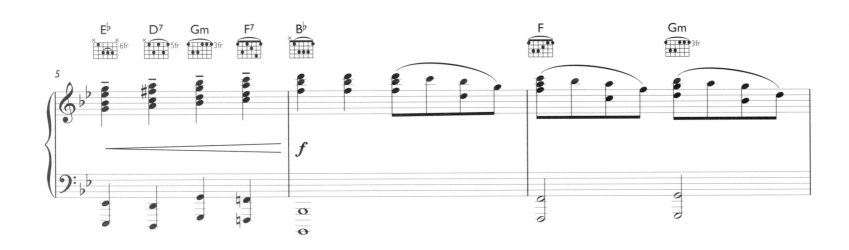

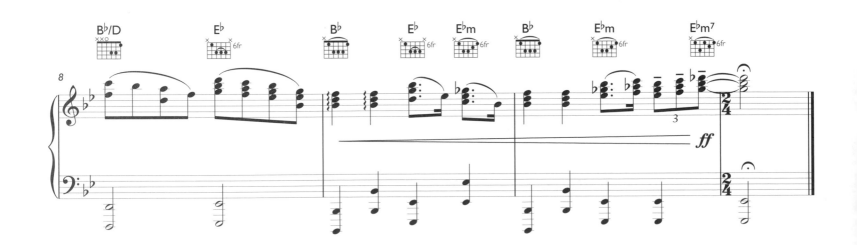

SURVIVAL

Words and Music by Matthew Bellamy

mine,   and I won't give   in,   be - cause   I   choose to thrive,   yes   I'm gon-na

win._____

(Fight,   fight,   fight,   fight,   win,   win,

win,   win.) Yes,   I'm   gon-na   win.

molto rit.

FOLLOW ME

Words and Music by Matthew Bellamy

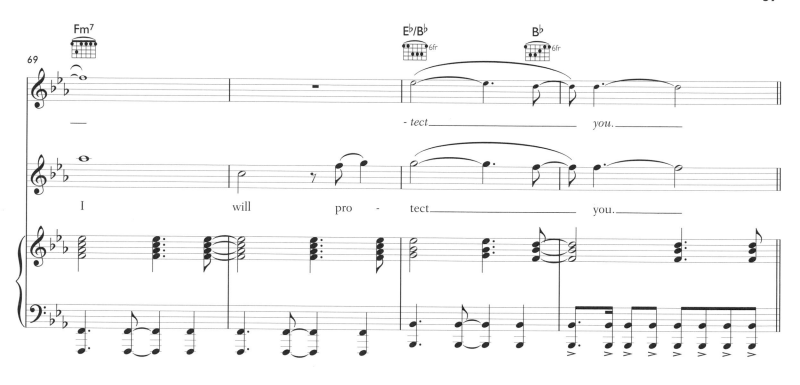

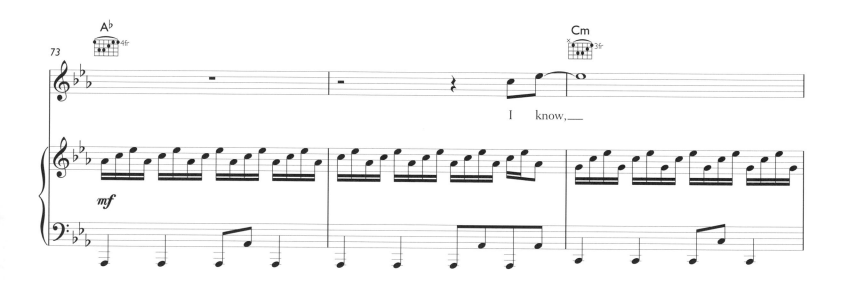

(Ah,_____ ah,_____

Fol - low_ me,_____ you can_ fol - low_ me,_____

ah,_____

I will al - ways keep_ you_____ safe._

Fol - low_ me,_____ you can_ trust in me,_____

ah,_____ ah,_____

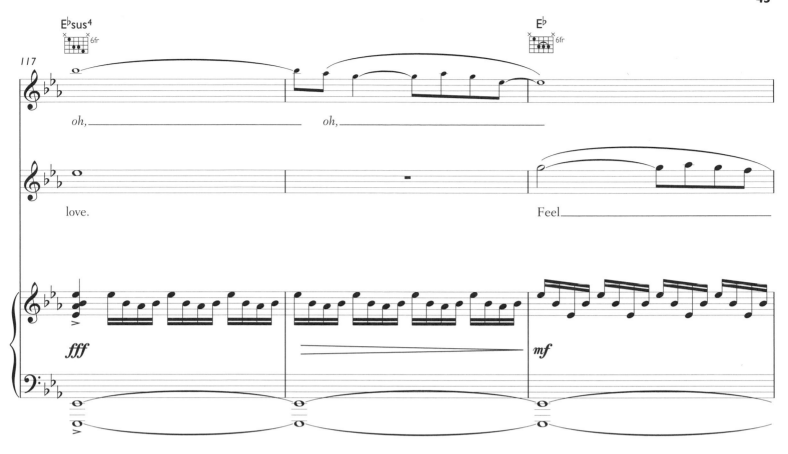

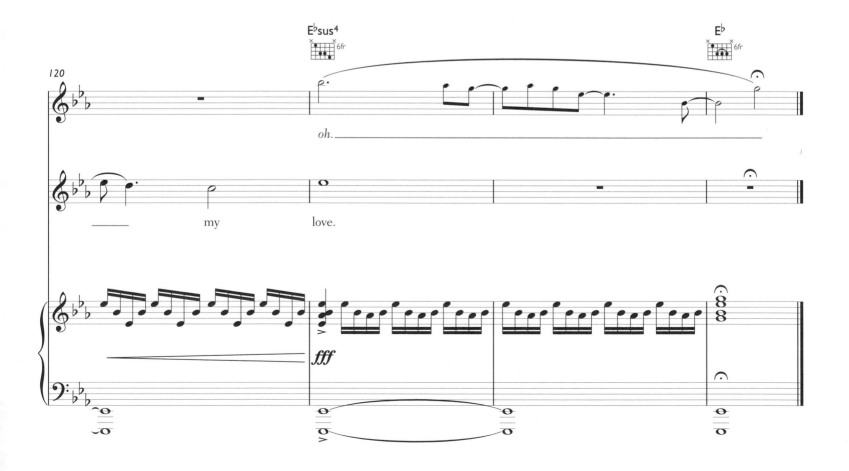

ANIMALS

Words and Music by Matthew Bellamy

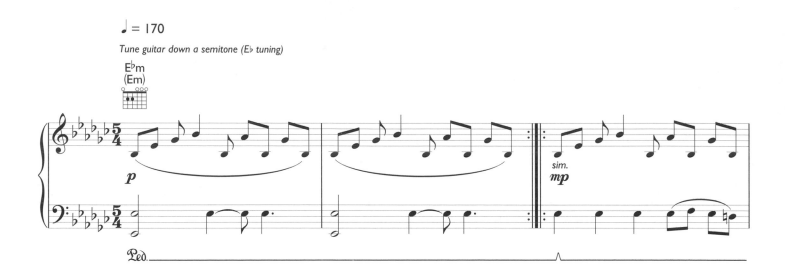

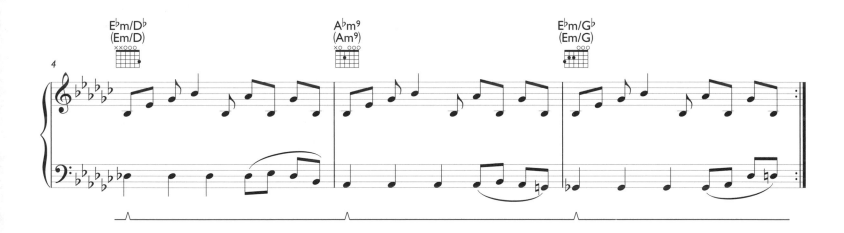

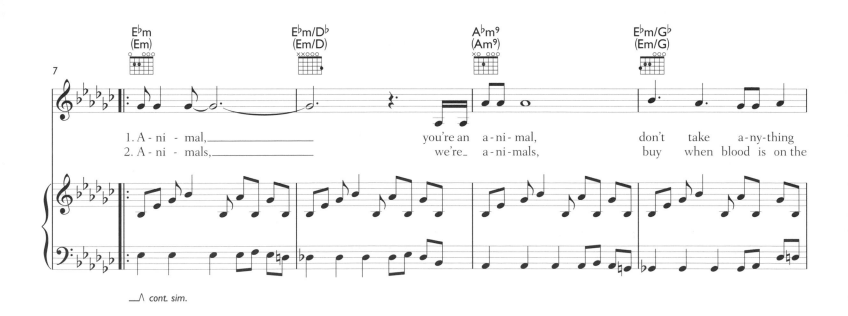

1. A-ni-mal,_____ you're an a-ni-mal, don't take a-ny-thing
2. Animals,_____ we're a-ni-mals, buy when blood is on the

Λ cont. sim.

less._____
street._____

Out of con - trol,_____   you're out of con - trol,___   strike those in dis -
Out of con - trol,_____   we're out of con - trol,___   crush those who beg at your

- tress._____
feet._____

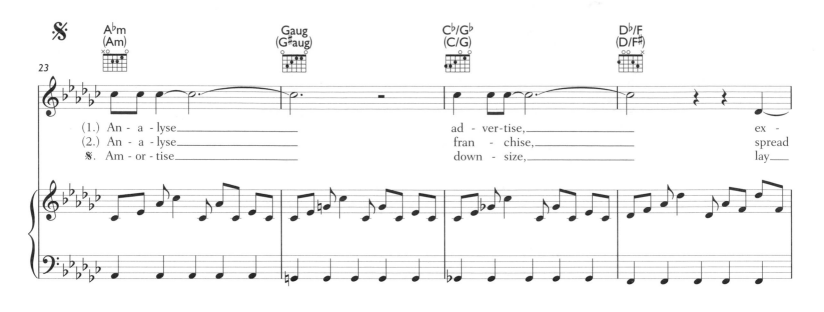

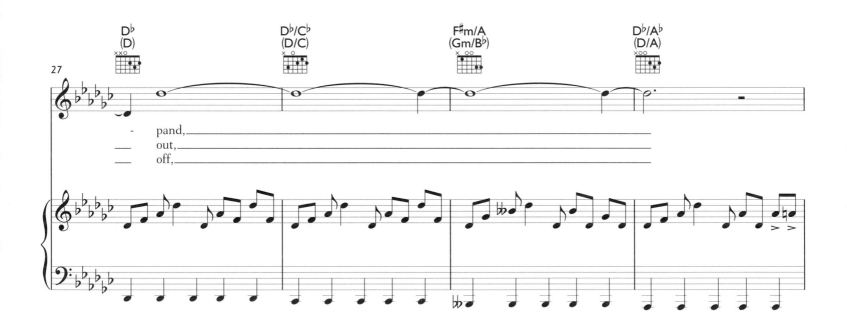

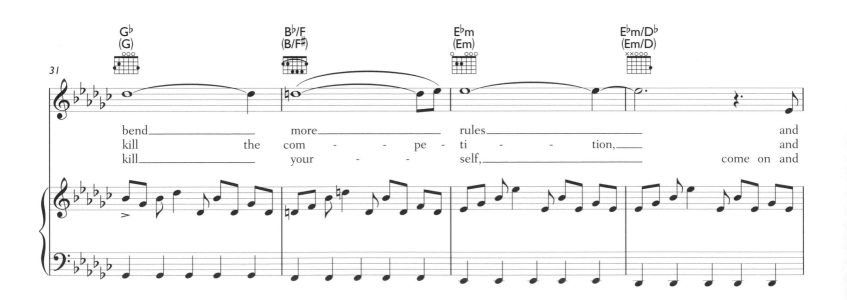

E♭7sus4
(E7sus4)

N.C.

Wall Street trading floor samples

EXPLORERS

Words and Music by Matthew Bellamy

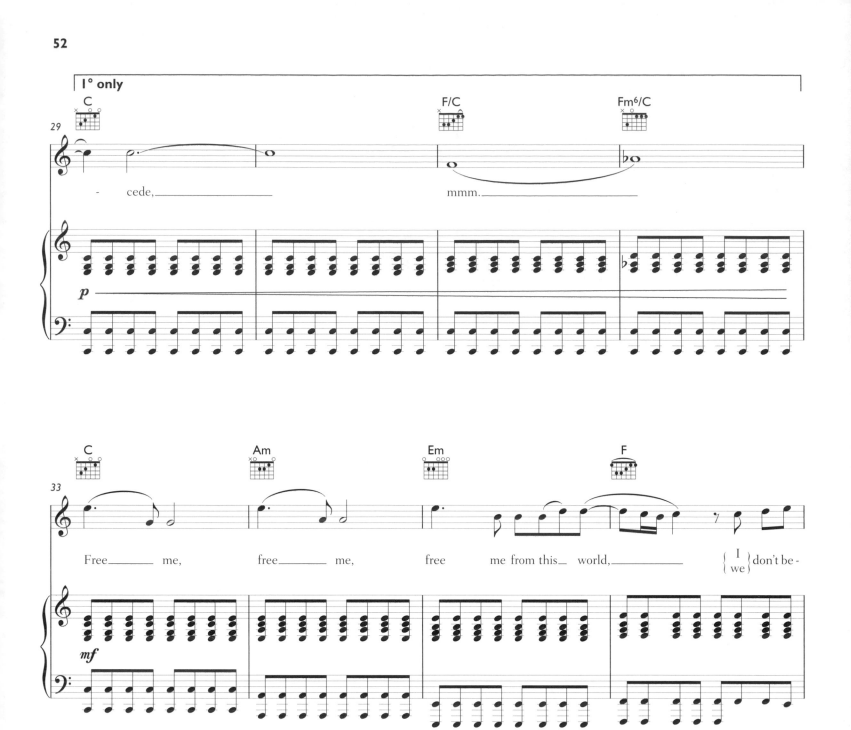

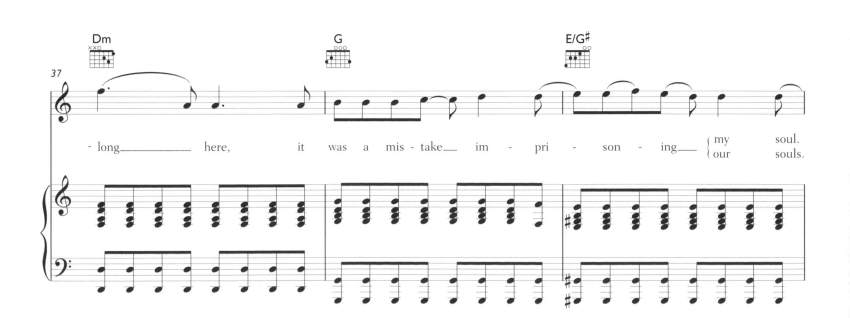

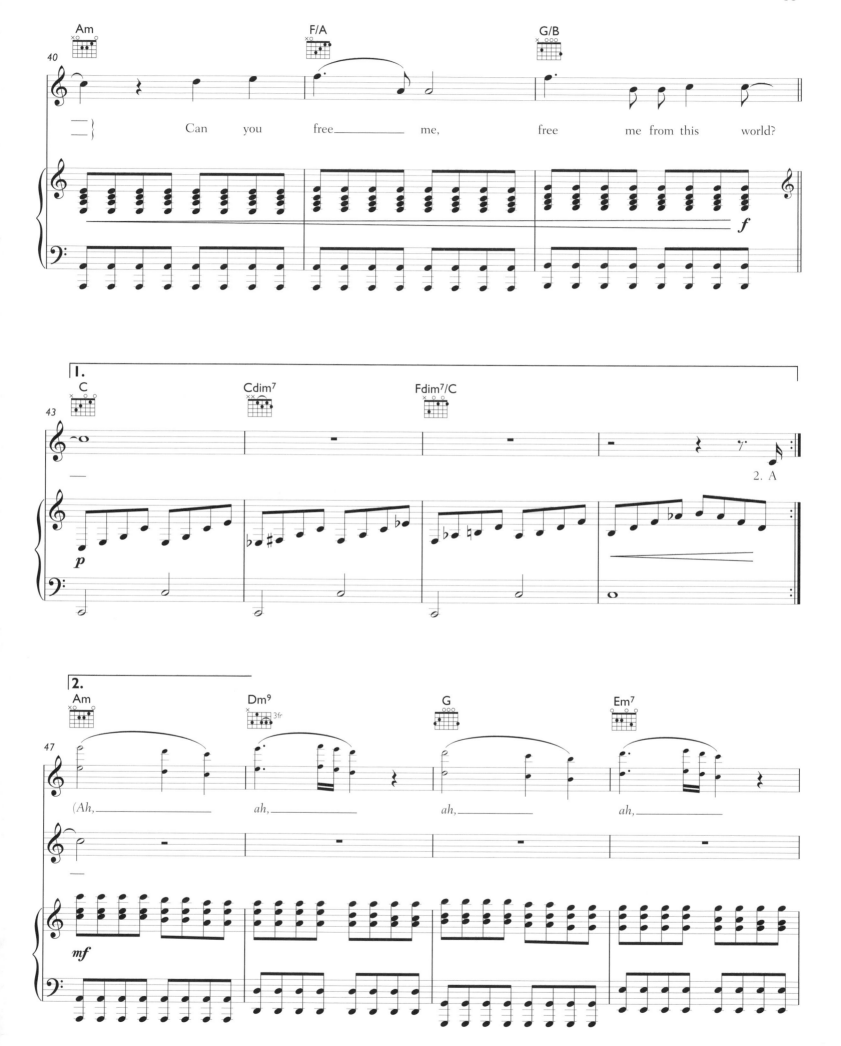

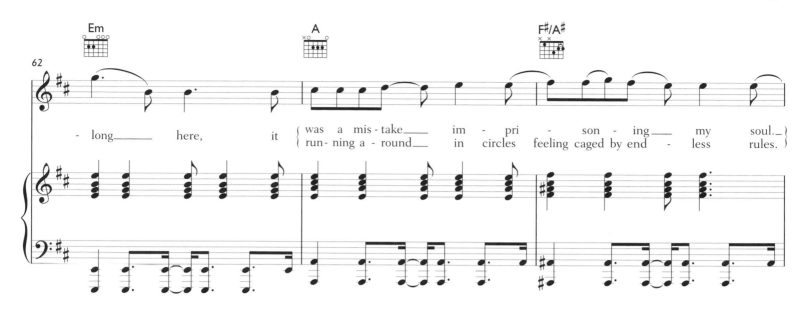

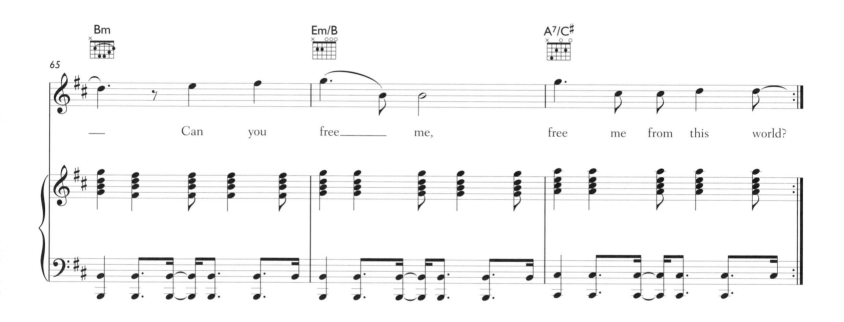

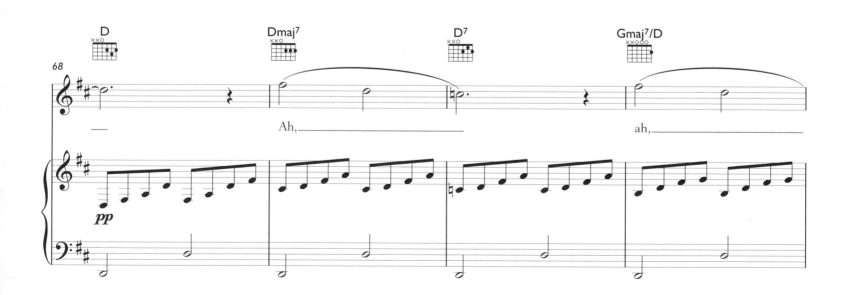

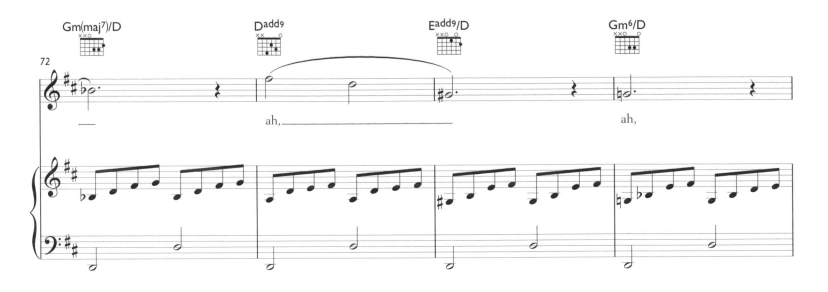

BIG FREEZE

Words and Music by Matthew Bellamy

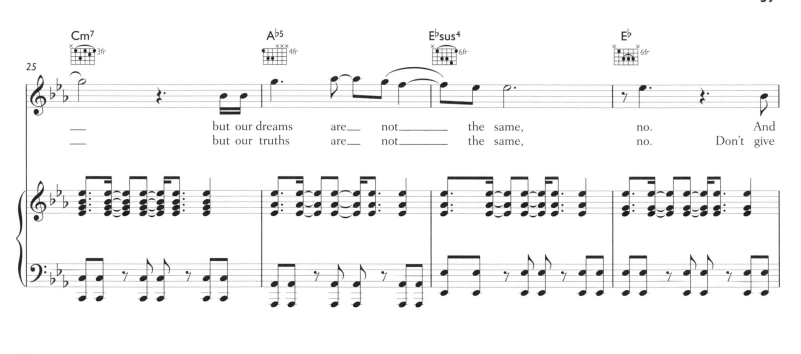

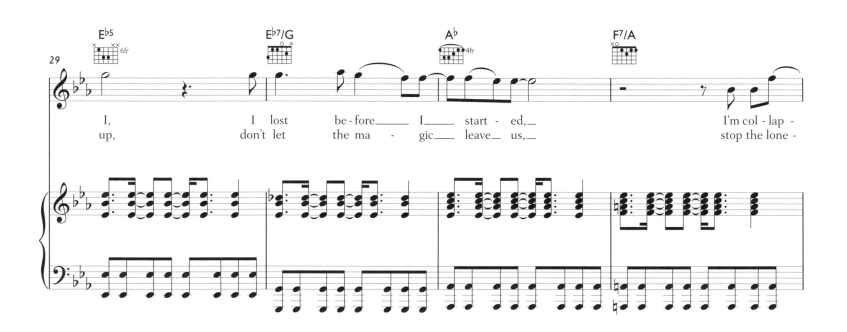

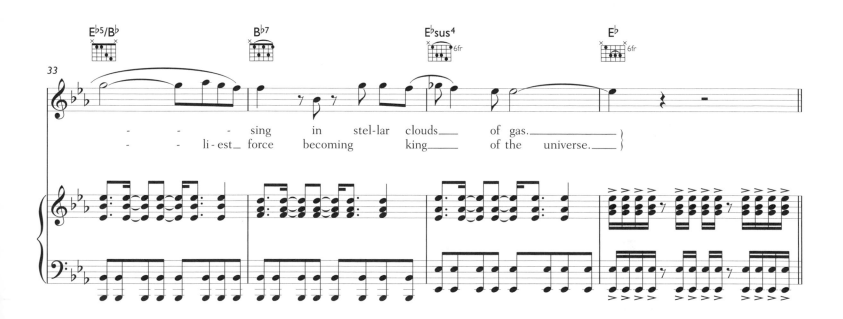

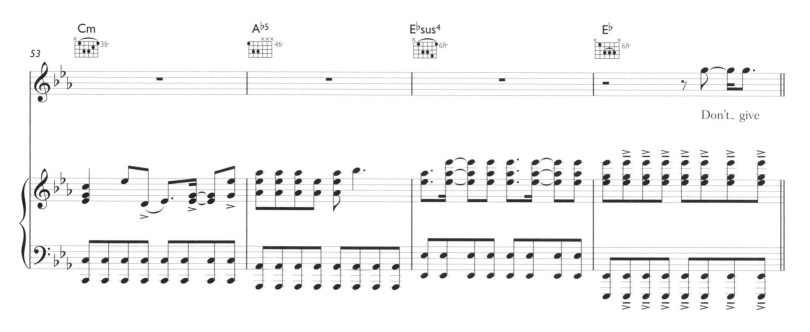

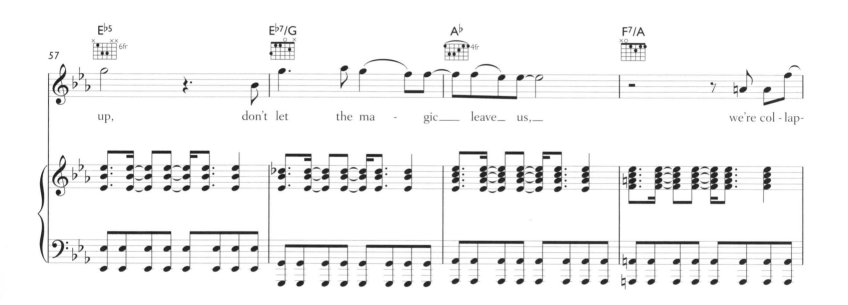

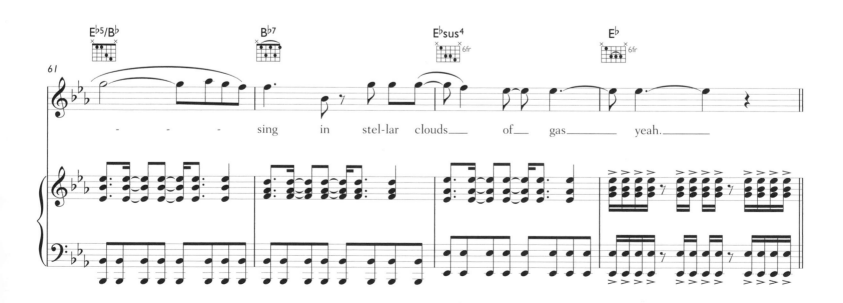

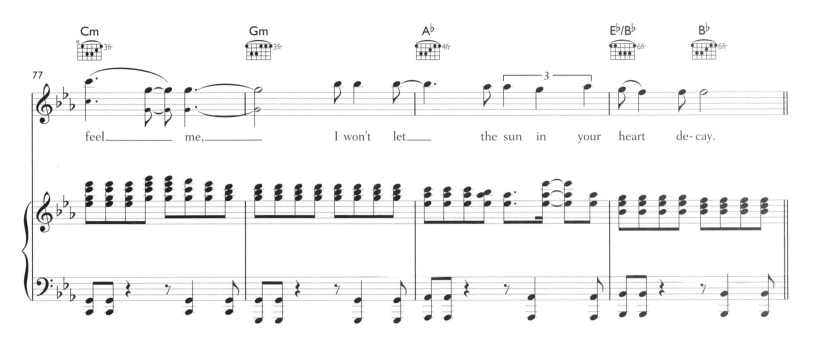

feel_____ me,_____ I won't let____ the sun in your heart de-cay.

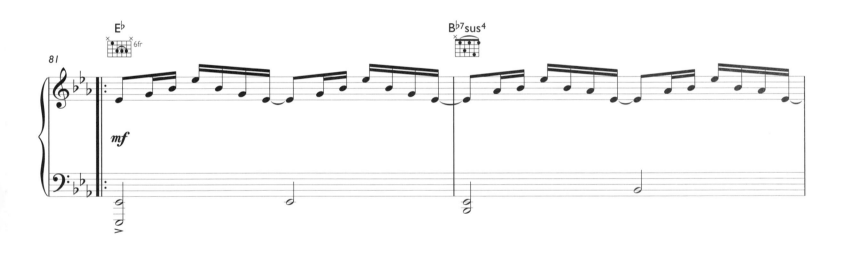

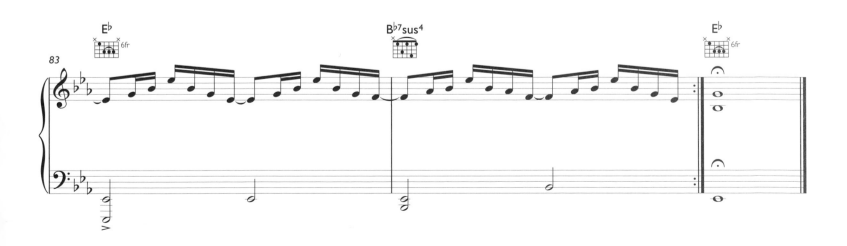

SAVE ME

Words and Music by Chris Wolstenholme

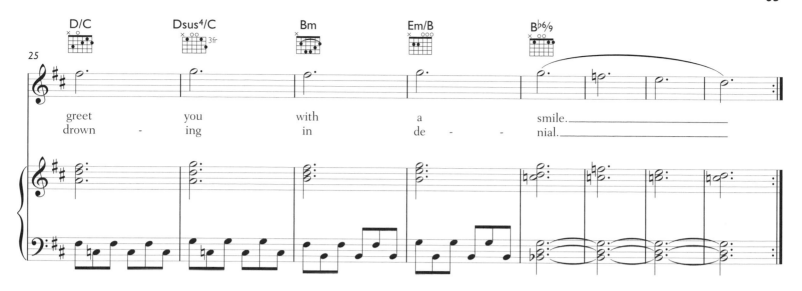

greet   you   with   a   smile._____
drown - ing   in   de -   nial._____

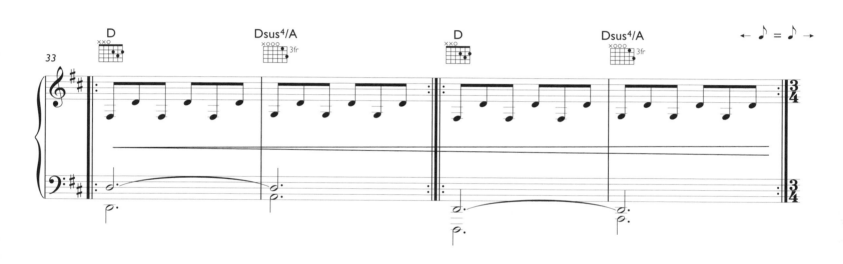

2. (Run   a -   - way   and

1. Turn   me   in -   - to
2. Run   a -   - way   and

mf   *sim.*

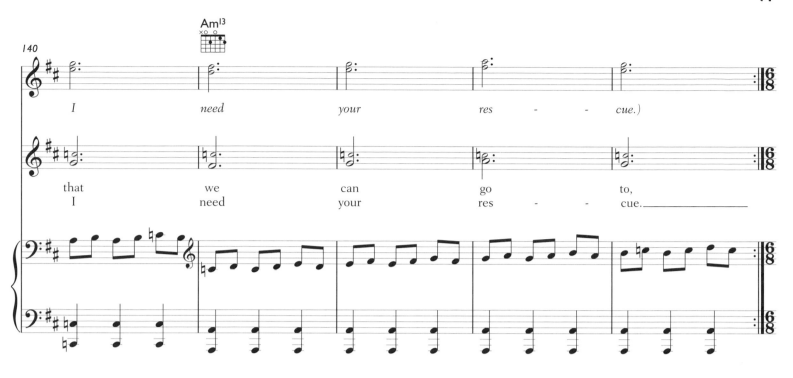

I need your res - cue.)

that we can go to,
I need your res - cue.____

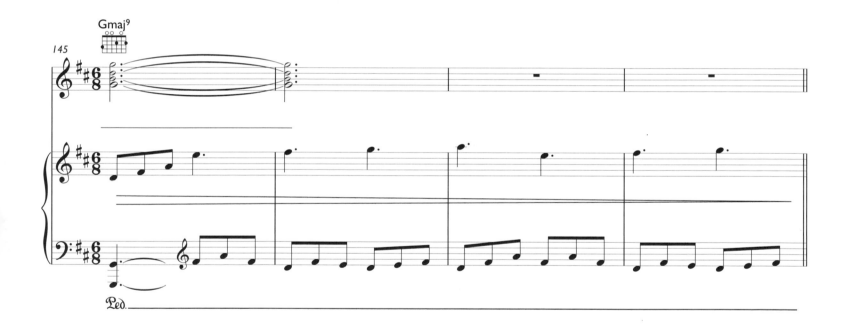

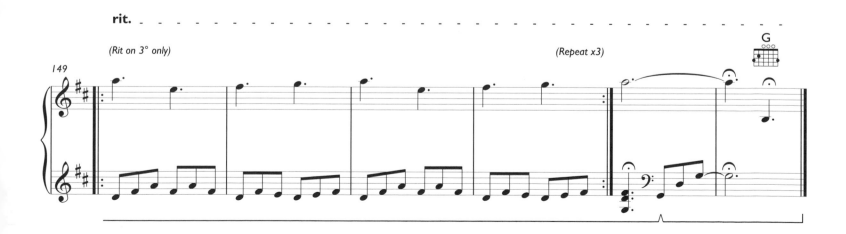

rit. - - - - - - - - - - - - -

(Rit on 3° only)

(Repeat x3)

LIQUID STATE

Words and Music by Chris Wolstenholme

2. I'm on red a- lert, bring me peace and wash a- way my
3. Kick me when I'm down, feed me poi- son, fill me till I

dirt, spin me round and help me to di-
drown, wake me up be- fore I get

- vert, and walk in- to the
pushed out and fall in- to the

light.
night.

gliss.

Ped.

THE 2ND LAW: UNSUSTAINABLE

Words and Music by Matthew Bellamy

(Spoken:) *"All virtual and technological processes proceed in such a way that the availability of the*

remaining energy decreases. In all energy exchanges, if no energy enters or leaves an isolated system

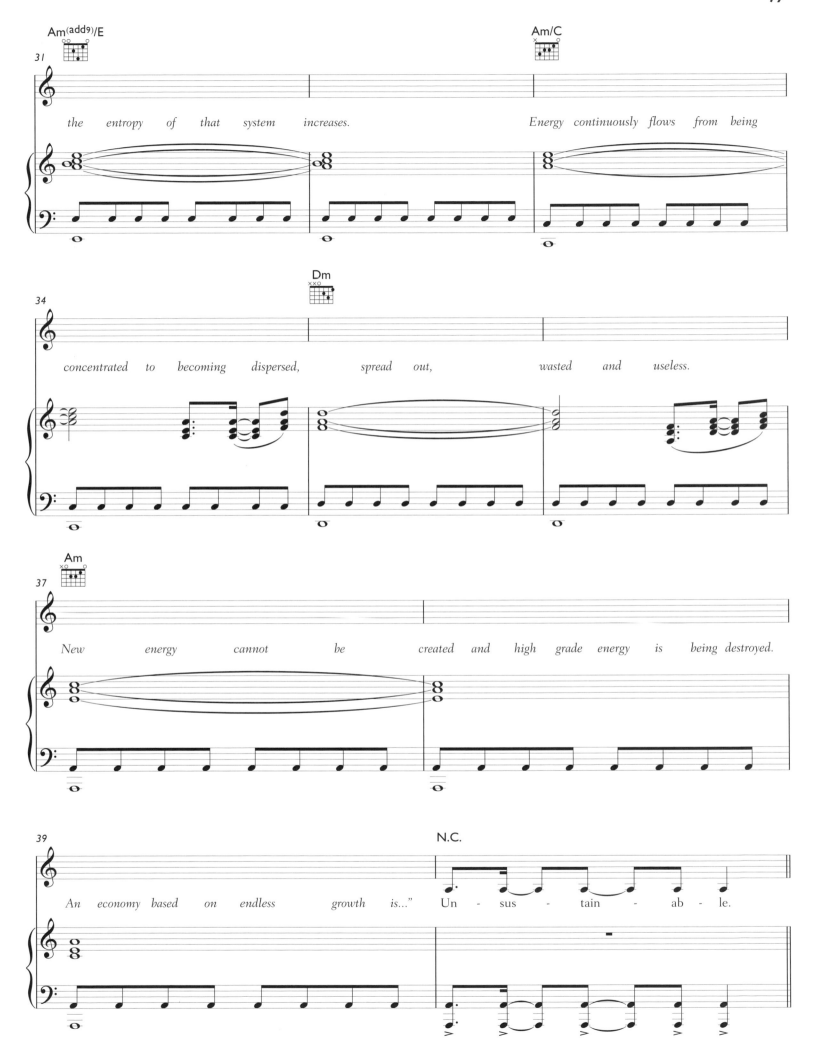

(Spoken:) *"The*

fundamental laws of thermodynamics will place fixed limits on technological innovation and human advancement.

THE 2ND LAW: ISOLATED SYSTEM

Words and Music by Matthew Bellamy

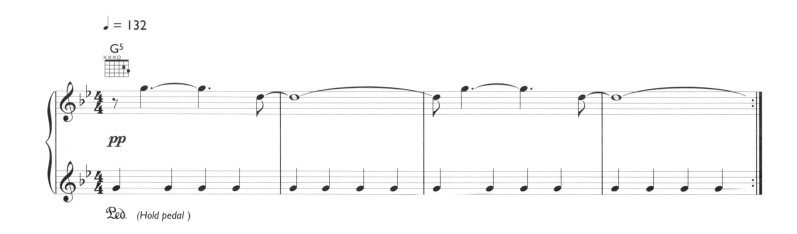

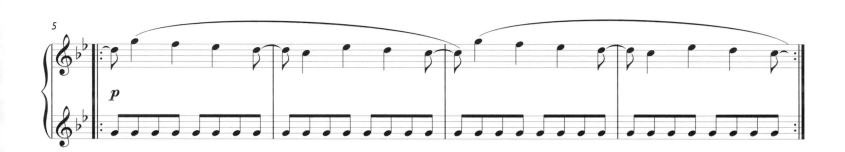

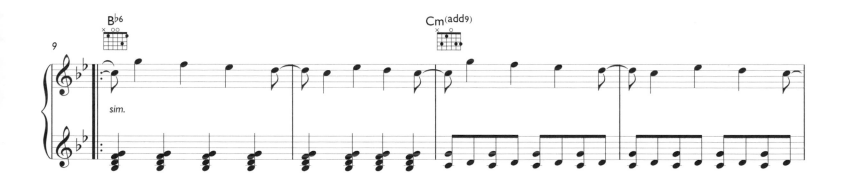

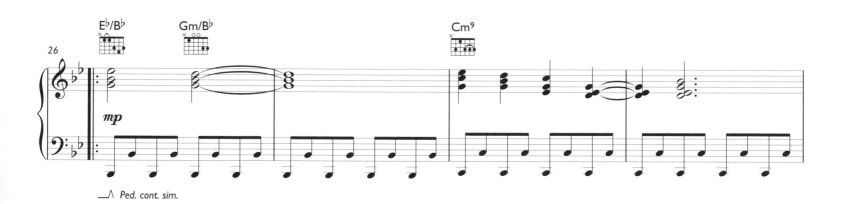